THE DANIEL STUDY

STUDY

Family/Children's Study

Angie Meadows

But Daniel resolved not to defile himself… Daniel 1:8

Thousand Tears, LLC, A
PO Box 1373
Huntington, WV 25715

Table of Contents

The DAniel Study 1

Lesson 1... 2

Daniel's Daring Decision 2

    Character Skill.. 3

    Standing Alone Evaluation 8

    Parent/Teacher Training 9

Lesson 2 10

Nebuchadnezzar's Dream of World Empires..................... 10

    Character Skill... 11

    Honoring Authority Evaluation 17

    Parents/Teachers Training............................... 18

Lesson 3 19

Deliverance From the Fiery Furnace 19

    Character Skill.. 20

    Physical Symptom of Fear 25

    Parent/Teacher Training 25

Lesson 4 27

The Humbling of Nebuchadnezzar............................... 27

    Character Skill.. 28

    Self-Evaluation.. 35

    PRIDE 35

    Humility.. 36

    Parent/Teacher Training 36

Lesson 5 38

The Handwriting on the Wall...................................... 38

    Character Skill.. 39

    HEART EVALUATION.. 44

Lesson 6 46

Daniel in the Lions' Den 46

    Character Skill...47

Feeble Faith...53

Healthy Faith...53

    Parent/Teacher Training 54

SALVATION PATHWAY..55

LESSON 1

DANIEL'S DARING DECISION

But Daniel resolved (purposed in his heart) not to defile himself with the royal food and wine... Daniel 1:8

Read:
Daniel 1:1-21

Principle: Culture can change your name, but it will never have the power to change your character when you honor and obey

---

Who:
The Prophet Daniel and his three friends: Hananiah, Mishael, and Azariah.
King of Judah: Jehoiakim
King of Babylon: Nebuchadnezzar
Master of the Eunuchs: Ashpenaz

When:
Third year of the reign of Jehoiakim King of Judah. 605BC

Where: Judah was the southern kingdom of Israel in the middle east.

What happened:

1) Jerusalem was invaded by Babylon, and they were taken captive and marched 500 miles from Jerusalem to Babylon. Ten thousand Jews were taken captive. 597BC The city and temple were destroyed. 586BC

2) The royal Jewish young men who had no blemish, well-favored, skillful in all wisdom and cunning in knowledge and understanding science and can learn quickly and easily are to be brought as captives to the Babylonian King's palace to become his wise men.

Why: Jehoiakim was an ungodly king of Judah and led the people into apostasy and persecuted the prophet Jeremiah and other true believers.

Vocabulary:

Apostasy is a refusal to follow, obey or recognize a religious faith. An abandonment of God and a leading of the people astray into idolatry.

Character Skill

Honor vs Disrespect

"Honor your father and your mother which is the first commandment with a promise—That it may go well with you and that you may enjoy long life on the earth.". *Ephesians 6:2-3*

Questions

1. Who came to Jerusalem? Daniel 1:1

2. When did King Nebuchadnezzar come? Daniel 1:1

3. Who was responsible for the nation of Jerusalem and Jehoiakim, King of Judah, being captured? Daniel 1:2

4. Who did King Nebuchadnezzar order Ashpenaz, chief of his court officials, to bring to his palace? And then what was he to do? Daniel 1:3-4

5. What were the names of four of the young men that were captured and what were their Babylonian names? Daniel 1:6-7

6. What did Daniel resolve not to do? Daniel 1:8

7. Who influenced the official to show Daniel favor and sympathy? Daniel 1: 9

8. What respectful appeal did Daniel ask of the chief official? Daniel 1:12-14

9. How did God bless these four young men for their desire to serve Him? Daniel 1:17

10. How much smarter were God's servants than the magicians and enchanters? Daniel 1:20

Answers
1. Nebuchadnezzar, King of Babylon.
2. Nebuchadnezzar came in the third year of the reign of Jehoiakim King of Judah.
3. God
4. Ashpenaz was to capture and bring in some of the young men from the royal family and others who were without physical defect, handsome, showing aptitude for every kind of learning, well informed, quick to understand and qualified to serve in the king's palace. Then Ashpenaz was to teach them the language and literature of the Babylonians.
5. Daniel, Hananiah, Mishael, and Azariah. They were renamed Belteshazzar, Shadrach, Meshach, Abednego.
6. Daniel resolved not to defile himself with the royal food and wine.
7. God

8. Daniel asked for just vegetables to eat and water to drink and to be tested for ten days, then for the official to compare them to the others and then Daniel submitted to Ashpenaz's judgment at the end of ten days.
9. To these four young men God gave knowledge and understanding of all kinds of literature and learning. And Daniel could understand visions and dreams of all kinds.
10. King Nebuchadnezzar found the Hebrew boys to be ten times smarter than his trained magicians and enchanters.

Challenge:

1. Discover what the boy's names meant in the Jewish language.

    Daniel-

    Hananiah-

    Mishael-

    Azariah

    Discover the meaning of their new names in the Babylonian language.

    Belteshazzar-

    Shadrach-

    Meshach-

    Abednego-

2. Look up other verses on authority and write a question and find the answer.
    Proverbs 21:1

Psalm 75:7

Romans 13:1

Hebrews 13:17

Challenge Answers to question 1 & 2:

Daniel means *God is judge.*
Renamed **Belteshazzar** means Bel will protect.
Hananiah means *God is gracious.*
Renamed **Shadrach** means inspiration of the sun.
Mishael means *God is without equal.*
Renamed **Meshach**, belonging to Aku, the moon god.
Azariah means *the Lord is my helper.*
Renamed **Abednego** means servant of Nego, the god of science and literature.

Discussion

1) What do you think might have happened if Daniel would have broken Jewish law and defiled himself with the king's food and wine?

2) How do you think the Hebrew boys handled the loss of their family, home, and the future kingdom of Judah?

Standing Alone Evaluation	
1. Do I have beliefs I am willing to stand for and be persecuted?	
2. Do I cower in fear when I am mocked or made fun of by my peers?	
3. Have I purposed in my heart to follow Christ, no matter what?	
4. Do I gravitate to friends that tear down and talk bad about our authorities?	
5. Do I know how to clear up a guilty conscience when I fail and become a rock to doing what is right next time? Do I confess quickly?	
6. Am I afraid of angry people?	
7. Do you lead others to obey God or follow wicked leaders?	
8. If you are given a command to lie, cheat or steal, are you willing to take a stand and refuse to do it?	

9. What disciplines could you set up in your life so you will be prepared to say no to evil?	
10. Have you developed strong friendships with honorable friends? And do you encourage them to become stronger or weaker in their resolve to do good?	

Parent/Teacher Training

1) **Stand Alone** like Daniel

In today's world, we must teach our children to stand alone. Stand one child in front of the room and role play. Have someone attempt to give the child a pretend cigarette, drink of alcohol or drug or to try to entice the child to cheat, lie or steal. With each temptation the child is to say: "you can do what you want, but I will not follow."

2) **Respect Authority** with first time obedience

Practice giving instruction and have the child move quickly to obey the first time. Do this 2-3 times a day for practice until the habit is developed. Obedience without a happy heart is obedience without honor. Have them repeat the lesson until they can obey with a smile.

3) **Make a Respectful Appeal**

A respectful appeal is taught after the child has learned to consistently obey the first time. This is what Daniel did. He would give new information and ask to be tested on his way of doing things and leave the outcome to God. He did this twice. Once with the food with Ashpenaz. And the second time to escape execution and give him time to interpret the dream in chapter 2 with Arioch, the commander of the king's guard.

LESSON 2

NEBUCHADNEZZAR'S DREAM OF WORLD EMPIRES

There is a God in heaven who reveals mysteries. Daniel 2:28

Read:
Daniel 2:1-49

Principle: Anger brings dominance, harshness and over corrects.

Who:
King Nebuchadnezzar's wise men: Babylonian magicians, enchanters, sorcerers, and astrologers along with Daniel and his three friends.
Arioch, the commander of the king's guard.

Vocabulary:
Prostrate is to be stretched out with your face on the ground in submission.

Character Skill

Obedience vs Willfulness

<u>True obedience is based on love.</u> *If you love me, you will obey what I command. And I will ask the Father, and he will give you another Counselor to be with you forever —The Spirit of truth.*

John 14:15-17 <u>True obedience leads to truth and the comfort of the Holy Spirit.</u>

<u>God reveals himself to those who love and obey him.</u> *Whoever has my commands and obeys them, he is the one who loves me. He who loves me will be loved by my Father, and I too will love him and show myself to him. John 14:21*

Questions

1. Who was King Nebuchadnezzar's counselor? Daniel 2:1

2. What was the impossible thing the king asked his advisors to do? Daniel 2:3-5a

3. What punishment for failure and what reward for success was Nebuchadnezzar offering his advisors for telling him his dream and interpreting it? Daniel 2:5b-6

4. In his fury, what did the King order to be done? Daniel 2:12-13

5. What two things did Daniel do when the commander of the king's guard came to kill him and his friends? Daniel 2:14-16

6. What was Daniel's respectful appeal? Daniel 2:15-16

7. Who did Daniel turn to? Daniel 2:17-18

8. Who did Daniel give glory to for his wisdom? Daniel 2:23,27-28

9. What was the dream and its meaning? Daniel 2:31-45 (Maybe you would like to draw instead of writing it.)

10. What happened to Daniel at the end of the chapter? Daniel 2:46-48

Answers

1. Magicians, enchanters, sorcerers, and astrologers.
2. You must tell me what my dream was and interpret it.
3. If you fail, I will have you cut into pieces and your houses turned into piles of rubble. But if you tell me the dream and explain it, you will receive from me gifts and rewards and great honor.
4. King Nebuchadnezzar ordered the execution of all the wise men of Babylon. This included Daniel and his friends.
5. A) Daniel responded with wisdom and tact.
   B) When Daniel learned of the situation, he calmly practiced making a respectful appeal.

6. A) Daniel gathered information, then he went to the king with a respectful appeal.

   B)   He asked the king for more time to interpret the dream.

7. He explained the situation to his three friends. Together they pleaded for mercy from the God of Heaven to reveal this mystery.

8. A) I thank and praise you, O God of my fathers: You have given me wisdom and power, you have made known to me what we asked of you, you have made known to us the dream of the king.

   B) Daniel replied: "No wise man, enchanter, magician, or diviner can explain to the king the mystery he has asked about but there is a God in heaven who reveals mysteries.

9. (31) You looked, O King, and there before you stood a large statue—an enormous, dazzling statue, awesome in appearance. (32) The head of the statue was made of pure gold, its chest and arms of silver, its belly, and thighs of bronze, (33) its legs of iron, its feet partly or iron and partly of baked clay. (34) While you were watching, a rock was cut out, but not by human hands. It struck the statue on its feet of iron and clay and smashed them. (35) Then the iron, the clay, the bronze, the silver, and the gold were broken to pieces at the same time and became like chaff on a threshing floor in the summer. The wind swept them away without leaving a trace. But the rock that struck the statue became a huge mountain and filled the whole earth. (36) This was the dream, and now we will interpret it to the king. (37) You, O King, are the king of kings, The God of the heaven has given you dominion and power and might and glory; (38) in your hands he has placed mankind and the beasts of the field and the birds of the air. Wherever they live, he has made you ruler over them all. You are that head of gold. (39) After you, another kingdom will rise, inferior to yours. Next, a third kingdom, one of bronze, will rule over the whole earth. (40) Finally, there will be a fourth kingdom, strong as iron—for iron breaks and smashes everything—as the iron breaks things to pieces, so it will crush and break all the others. (41) Just as you saw that the feet and toes were partly of baked clay and partly of iron, so this will be a divided kingdom: yet it will have some of the strength of iron in it, even as you saw iron mixed with clay. (42) As the toes were partly iron and partly clay, so this kingdom will be partly strong and partly brittle. (43) And just as you saw the iron mixed with baked clay, so the people will be a mixture and will not remain united, any more than iron mixes with clay. (44) In that time of those kings, the God of heaven will set up a kingdom that will never be destroyed, nor will it be left to another people. It will crush all those kingdoms and bring them to an end, but it will itself endure forever.

10. (46) The king fell prostate before Daniel and paid him honor and ordered that an offering and incense be presented to him. (47) Then the king honored Daniel's God. "Surely your God is the God of gods and the Lord of Kings and a revealer of mysteries, for you were able to reveal this mystery."
(48) Then Daniel was placed in a high position and lavished many gifts on him. The king made him ruler over the entire province of Babylon and placed him in charge of all its wise men. (49) Then at Daniel's request, the king placed Shadrach, Meshach, and Abednego administrators over the province of Babylon, while Daniel himself remained at the royal court.

Challenge
In Daniel chapter 2 find reasons to praise God:

Challenge Answer
Reasons to Praise God

1. Wisdom belongs to God. (vs. 20)
2. Power belongs to God. (vs.20)
3. God changes the times and seasons. (vs. 21)
4. God sets up kings. (vs. 21)
5. God gives wisdom to the wise. (vs. 21)
6. God gives knowledge to those with understanding. (vs. 21)
7. God reveals deep secret things. He knows what is in the darkness and the light dwells with him. (vs. 22)
8. We can thank God and praise him because he gives us wisdom and might and makes known to us what we desire to know and reveals to us things our leader's need to know. (vs. 23)

Discussion

1) Why do you think King Nebuchadnezzar was so unreasonable?

2) Why do you think Daniel was so calm when his life was in danger?

3) Do you think that Nebuchadnezzar got prideful when he realized he was the head of gold in the dream?

Honoring Authority Evaluation

1. Do you challenge obedience?

2. Do you obey disgruntled?

3. Do you complain when asked to do a job you don't want to do?

4. Do you make excuses?

5. After one parent says no, does your child go to the other parent?

6. Is the family united, or is there one person that is allowed to divide the family with anger or tears or other strong emotions?

7. Are you slow to follow instructions?

8. Do you pretend you didn't understand or didn't hear instructions?

9. Do you nag after you are told "no", until you relent and change your mind?
10. Do you do everything to your best ability as unto the Lord and not unto man?

Parents/Teachers Training

1. You want children to develop values and opinions. We do not want robot children that can't think and just do whatever they are told.

Peter says, "we ought to obey God rather than man." Acts 5:29

---

2. Teach your children when they are to disobey. They are to disobey if someone is asking them to lie, cheat, steal or do something wrong or harmful to another. Then they are to trust God with the outcome, no matter what!

LESSON 3

DELIVERANCE FROM THE FIERY FURNACE

But even if he (God) does not (deliver us), we want you to know, O King, that we will not serve your gods or worship the image of gold you have set up. Daniel 3:18

Read:
Daniel 3:1–30

Principle Right living gives us confidence to follow God.

Who:
King Nebuchadnezzar, Shadrach, Meshach, and Abednego. All the princes, governors, captains, judges, treasurers, counselors, sheriffs, and rulers of the province waited expectantly. The king's army stood nearby. The musicians were ready.

Where:
The statue was set up in the plain of Dura about 6 miles from Babylon.

Why:
The dream of being the head of gold may have elevated Nebuchadnezzar's opinion of himself.

What happened:
Nebuchadnezzar built a 90-foot tall and 9-foot-wide statue and had all the dignitaries and people gather to worship it. As the king, he required everyone to bow to the statute or to be thrown into the fiery furnace.

Vocabulary:
Glorify is to bestow honor, praise, or admiration.

Character Skill

Boldness vs Fear
Boldness welcomes persecution for doing what is right. *The righteous are as bold as lions. Proverbs 28:1*

It is a command to "fear not". Practice recognizing fear and instead exercising your faith. *Fear not, for I am with you...Isaiah 43:5*

They overcame him by the blood of the Lamb, and by the Word of their testimony; and they loved not their lives unto the death. Revelation 12:11 Boldness is based on my love for God even unto death.

Questions
1. What did Nebuchadnezzar build and how big was it? Daniel 3:1

2. What was Nebuchadnezzar's command? Daniel 3:4-5

3. What was the consequence of disobedience? Daniel 3:6

4. What question did Nebuchadnezzar ask them? Daniel 3:14

5. How do you know Nebuchadnezzar thought he was more powerful than God? Daniel 3:15

6. What did the three Hebrew boys say to the king? Daniel 3:16-17

7. Were the three Hebrew boys more concerned with saving their lives or obeying God and trusting him with the outcome? Daniel 3:18

8. What happened to the men who obeyed the king and threw three righteous Hebrew boys into the fiery furnace? Daniel 3:22

9. Who did the king see in the fiery furnace with the Hebrew boys? Daniel 3:25

10. How did God glorify the three Hebrew boys? Daniel 3:27b; 30

11. How did God glorify himself through the obedience of three Hebrew boys? Daniel 3:28-29

Answers

1. Nebuchadnezzar built a gold statue that was 90 feet high and 9 feet wide.
2. Then the herald loudly proclaimed, "This is what you are commanded to do, O peoples, nations, and men of every language. As soon as you hear the sound of the horn, flute, zither, lyre, harp, pipes, and all kinds of music, you must fall down and worship the image of gold that King Nebuchadnezzar has set up."
3. "Whoever does not fall down, and worship will immediately be thrown into a blazing furnace."
4. And Nebuchadnezzar said to them, "Is it true, Shadrach, Meshach, and Abednego, that you do not serve my gods or worship the image of gold I have set up?
5. Now when you hear the sound of the horn, flute, zither, lyre, harp, pipes and all kinds of music, if you are ready to fall down and worship the image I. made, then it is very good. But if you do not worship it, you will be thrown immediately into a blazing furnace. Then what god will be able to rescue you from my hand?
6. Shadrach, Meshach, and Abednego replied to the king, "O Nebuchadnezzar, we do not need to defend ourselves before you in this matter. If we are thrown into the blazing furnace, the God we serve is able to save us from it, and he will rescue us from your hand, O king.
7. But even if he does not, we want you to know, O king, that we will not serve your gods or worship the image of gold you have set up.
8. The king's command was so urgent and the furnace so hot that the flames of the fire killed the soldiers who took up Shadrach, Meshach, and Abednego.
9. He (Nebuchadnezzar) said, "Look! I see four men walking around in the fire, unbound and unharmed, and the fourth looks like a son of the gods."
10. They (the people, leaders) saw the fire had not harmed their bodies, nor was a hair of their heads singed; their robes were not scorched, and there was no smell of fire on them. Then the king promoted Shadrach, Meshach, and Abednego in the province of Babylon.
11. Then Nebuchadnezzar said, "Praise be to the God of Shadrach, Meshach, and Abednego, who has sent his angel and rescued his servants! They trusted in him and defied the king's command and were willing to give up their lives rather than serve or worship any god except their own God. Therefore, I decree that the people of any nation or language who say anything against the God of Shadrach, Meshach and Abednego be cut into pieces and their houses be turned into piles of rubble, for no other god can save in this way.

Challenge

1. Recognize when you are afraid of a person. *Fear of man will prove to be a snare, but whoever trusts in the LORD is kept safe. Proverbs 29:25*

2. The fear of the Lord is the beginning of wisdom. Ask God to give you a reverential fear of him that is powerful enough to choose to do right. *The fear of the LORD is the beginning of knowledge, but fools despise wisdom and instruction. Proverbs 1:7*

3. Challenge the children to look for opportunities to stand alone and not follow peer pressure. *Now Daniel purposed in his heart that he would not defile himself... Daniel 1:8*

Discussion

1. If you submit to an unreasonable man, who asks you to make a compromise how do you think this will turn out?

2. How can you tell if a person worships themselves? (See Luke 18:9-14. Who did he praise? Who did he put down?)

3. Why do you think Nebuchadnezzar's servants told on the three Hebrew boys?

4. Do you think the Hebrew boys answered the king respectfully?

Physical Symptom of Fear	
1. Teeth grinding	
2. Jaw tightening	
3. Racing/uncontrollable thoughts	
4. No thoughts	
5. Freezing unable to move	
6. Pain/Physical	
7. Heart rate increased	
8. Sweating	
9. Choking food/water	
10. Twitching	
11. Nail/lip biting	
12. Picking/scratching at skin	
13. Bowel issues	
14. Restlessness	
15. Sleeplessness	
16. Drowsiness/unable to get off couch	
17. Overeating	
18. Undereating	
19. Self-destructive	
Obsessing over games/computer	
Overworking	

Parent/Teacher Training

1. Practice boldness. Role play what it would look like to be bullied to do something wrong. Talk about peer pressure and how to stand alone when you are persecuted for doing right or for refusing to do what is wrong. *Woe to those who call evil good and good evil... Isaiah 5:20*

> *You shall love the Lord your God with all your heart and*
> *with all your soul and with all your mind and with all your strength.*
> *Mark 12:30*

2. Teach the principle that when we follow and obey God with our whole heart, soul, and mind, we are indestructible until God is done with us. Our lives wil be steadfast in serving him day in and day out.

3. When you follow Jesus Christ and not ungodly authority, they may be seven times angrier at you. Ungodly leaders lead with bullying and fear. Godly leaders lead with a heart of servanthood. What type of a leader do you want to be when you grow up?

LESSON 4

THE HUMBLING OF NEBUCHADNEZZAR

Read:
Daniel 4:1–37

Principle: Pride takes a man's reason.

Who: Nebuchadnezzar, the gentile King of Babylon, wrote this chapter in the Bible.

When: From about 606 or 616 to 536BC

Where: Babylon

Why: God sets up kings and takes them down. The humbling of King Nebuchadnezzar shows how God corrects the prideful and elevates the humble.

What happened: Nebuchadnezzar refused to heed the warning of the dream of the tree. He did not take Daniel's advice and repent for his pride or have compassion for the poor. God gave him a year to repent. Nebuchadnezzar was driven to the fields with the mind of a beast to act like an animal for 7 years. When the time was over, he lifted his eyes and acknowledged the one true God.

Character Skill

Pride vs Humility

Humility is total dependency on the Lord and seeking his will in every decision.

All of you, <u>clothe</u> yourselves with <u>humility</u> toward one another, because "God opposes the proud but shows favor to the humble." Humble yourselves, therefore, under God's mighty hand, that he may lift you up in due time. 1 Peter 5:5-6

Pride reserves the right to make my own decisions based upon my selfish needs.

Humility is the fear of the LORD; its wages are riches and honor and life. Proverbs 22:4

Questions

1. Nebuchadnezzar starts chapter 4 with an introduction. What was his praise to God in Daniel 4:3?

2. Nebuchadnezzar describes himself as content and prosperous. Then he said he was terrified. What terrified King Nebuchadnezzar? Daniel 4:4-5

3. Who did Nebuchadnezzar tell the dream to first and could they interpret it? Daniel 4:7

4. When Daniel arrived, who did Nebuchadnezzar say was in Daniel? Daniel 4:8-9

5. Describe Nebuchadnezzar's dream? Daniel 4:10-18

6. What did the king say to Daniel to comfort him? Daniel 4:19

7. What was Daniel's interpretation? Daniel 4:19b-26

8. What were Daniel's suggestions to Nebuchadnezzar? Daniel 4:27

9. What happened 12 months later because of Nebuchadnezzar's lack of repentance of his pride? Daniel 28-33

10. What was Nebuchadnezzar's testimony after his seven years of exile to the field with the mind of an animal? Daniel 4: 34-36

Answers

1. How great are his signs, how mighty his wonders!
   His kingdom is an eternal kingdom.
   His dominion endures from generation to generation.
2. Nebuchadnezzar had another dream.
3. Nebuchadnezzar told the dream to his magicians, enchanters, astrologers, and diviners, but they could not interpret it.
4. Nebuchadnezzar said that the spirit of the holy gods was in Daniel.
5. Daniel 4:10-18 NIV These are the visions I saw while lying in bed: I looked, and there before me stood a tree in the middle of the land. Its height was enormous. [11] The tree grew large and strong, and its top touched the sky; it was visible to the ends of the earth. [12] Its leaves were beautiful, its fruit abundant, and on it was food for all. Under it the wild animals found shelter, and the birds lived in its branches; from it every creature was fed. [13] "In the visions I saw while lying in bed, I looked, and there before me was a holy one, a messenger, coming down from heaven. [14] He called in a loud voice: 'Cut down the tree and trim off its branches; strip off its leaves and scatter its fruit. Let the animals flee from under it and the birds from its branches. [15] But let the stump and its roots, bound with iron and bronze, remain in the ground, in the grass of the field. "'Let him be drenched with the dew of heaven and let him live with the animals among the plants of the earth. [16] Let his mind be changed from that of a man and let him be given the mind of an animal, till seven times pass by for him. [17] "'The decision is announced by messengers, the holy ones declare the verdict, so that the living may know that the Most High is sovereign over all kingdoms on earth and gives them to anyone he wishes and sets over them the lowliest of people.' [18] "This is the dream that I, King Nebuchadnezzar, had. Now, Belteshazzar, tell me what it means, for none of the wise men in my kingdom can interpret it for me. But you can, because the spirit of the holy gods is in you."

6. Daniel, also called Belteshazzar, thought's terrified him. The king said, "Belteshazzar, do not let the dream or its meaning alarm you."

7. Daniel 4:19-26 NIV Then Daniel (also called Belteshazzar) was greatly perplexed for a time, and his thoughts terrified him. So, the king said, "Belteshazzar, do not let the dream or its meaning alarm you." Belteshazzar answered, "My lord, if only the dream applied to your enemies and its meaning to your adversaries! [20] The tree you saw, which grew large and strong, with its top touching the sky, visible to the whole earth, [21] with beautiful leaves and abundant fruit, providing food for all, giving shelter to the wild animals, and having nesting places in its branches for the birds- [22] Your Majesty, you are that tree! You have become great and strong; your greatness has grown until it reaches the sky, and your dominion extends to distant parts of the earth. [23] "Your Majesty saw a holy one, a messenger, coming down from heaven and saying, 'Cut down the tree and destroy it, but leave the stump, bound with iron and bronze, in the grass of the field, while its roots remain in the ground. Let him be drenched with the dew of heaven; let him live with the wild animals, until seven times pass by for him.' [24] "This is the interpretation, Your Majesty, and this is the decree the Most High has issued against my lord the king: [25] You will be driven away from people and will live with the wild animals; you will eat grass like the ox and be drenched with the dew of heaven. Seven times will pass by for you until you acknowledge that the Most High is sovereign over all kingdoms on earth and gives them to anyone he wishes. [26] The command to leave the stump of the tree with its roots means that your kingdom will be restored to you when you acknowledge that Heaven rules.

8. Daniel 4:27 NIV Therefore, Your Majesty, be pleased to accept my advice: Renounce your sins by doing what is right, and your wickedness by being kind to the oppressed. It may be that then your prosperity will continue."

9. Daniel 4:28-33 NIV All this happened to King Nebuchadnezzar. [29] Twelve months later, as the king was walking on the roof of the royal palace of Babylon, [30] he said, "Is not this the great Babylon I have built as the royal residence, by my mighty power and for the glory of my majesty?" [31] Even as the words were on his lips, a voice came from heaven, "This is what is decreed for you, King Nebuchadnezzar: Your royal authority has been taken from you. [32] You will be driven away from people and will live with the wild animals; you will eat grass like the ox. Seven times will pass by for you until you acknowledge that the Most High is sovereign over all kingdoms on earth and gives them to anyone he wishes." [33] Immediately what had been said about Nebuchadnezzar was fulfilled. He was driven away from people and ate grass

like the ox. His body was drenched with the dew of heaven until his hair grew like the feathers of an eagle and his nails like the claws of a bird.

10. Daniel 4:34-37 NIV At the end of that time, I, Nebuchadnezzar, raised my eyes toward heaven, and my sanity was restored. Then I praised the Most High; I honored and glorified him who lives forever. His dominion is an eternal dominion; his kingdom endures from generation to generation. [35] All the peoples of the earth are regarded as nothing. He does as he pleases with the powers of heaven and the peoples of the earth. No one can hold back his hand or say to him: "What have you done?" [36] At the same time that my sanity was restored, my honor and splendor were returned to me for the glory of my kingdom. My advisers and nobles sought me out, and I was restored to my throne and became even greater than before. [37] Now I, Nebuchadnezzar, praise and exalt and glorify the King of heaven, because everything he does is right, and all his ways are just. And those who walk in pride he is able to humble.

Challenge

1. Can you find the things that Nebuchadnezzar learned? Which of these things do you need to learn and apply to your life?

2. If you were Nebuchadnezzar, would you have listened to the warnings in the dream? Do you listen to your parents and teachers' warnings?

Discussion

1. What was the root cause of Nebuchadnezzar being driven to the field and having his mind taken away from him?

2. If God gives a person great power, he also gives them the responsibility to care for others. What kind of a leader would you be? How do you lead younger siblings? Kind? Patient? Selfish? Cruel?

3. Why might Daniel be afraid to interpret the dream for Nebuchadnezzar?

4.   What might have happened if Nebuchadnezzar had repented?

Self-Evaluation

PRIDE	
1) Opinionated	
2) Stubborn	
3) Anxious	
4) Angry	
5) Immoral thinking or actions	
6) User	
7) Pouty	
8) Manipulative	
9) Demanding	
10) Controlling	
11) Doesn't repay	
12) Rails things we don't understand	
13) Judgmental	
14) Bitter	
15) Unforgiving	
16) Extorts from others	
17) Thinks of self very highly	
18) Indifference to the feelings of others	
19) Honors Self	

James 4:6 ... God opposes (resist) the proud but shows favor (gives grace) to the humble.

If you have pride, repent quickly.

Humility	
1) Kind	
2) Patient	
3) Speaks truth in love	
4) Waits for God to move first; doesn't force things	
5) Honors God in words and deeds	
6) Considers others better than themselves	
7) Doesn't think highly of self	
8) Complete dependency on God (manifested by a vibrant prayer life)	
No, I strike a blow to my body and make it my slave so that after I have preached to others, I myself will not be disqualified for the prize. 1 Corinthians 9:27 (Subject is Christian Liberty)	

Parent/Teacher Training

1. Differentiate between pride and humility. Pride will be bold to demand their own way with selfish motives. Humility will stand alone and stand strong with gentleness and firmness to always do what is right. No matter what the consequences.

2. Pay attention to your physical reaction when you are afraid of someone. Fear can cause a fight, flight, freeze or fawn response. Fear can come out as anger. *Fear of man will prove a snare, but whoever trusts in the LORD is kept safe. Proverbs 29:25*

Developing the skills to stand alone in humility with the motive to please God will make us bold in Christ.

---

3. People pleaser *Am I now trying to win the approval of human beings, or of God? Or am I trying to please people? If I were still trying to please people, I would not be a servant of Christ. Galatians 1:10*

4. *The fear of man lays a snare (trap), but whoever trusts in the LORD is safe. Proverbs 29:25* Identify and correct your fear of others or it will trap you in anxiety.

LESSON 5

THE HANDWRITING ON THE WALL

Read:
Daniel 5:1-31

Principle: Authority rises and falls by the hand of the Lord.
Psalm 75:7

Who: Belshazzar, was the son of Nabonidus and grandson of Nebuchadnezzar. He was second in command. The wisemen, Queen Mother most likely Nebuchadnezzar's wife and Belshazzar's grandmother, and Daniel, the prophet.

When: In the reign of Nabonidus. Belshazzar was in command over Babylon most likely he was away governing other parts of the kingdom.

Where: Babylon

What happened: Belshazzar was having a party and they were drunk. He commanded his servants to go and obtain the vessels of gold and silver from storage. Then Belshazzar defiled God's holy vessels with worship to false gods of gold, silver, brass, iron, wood, and stone. A finger appeared and wrote on the wall. Daniel prophesied the meaning of the message. Belshazzar's kingdom was divided and taken from him that night and he was killed. Darius, the Mede, took over the kingdom.

Character Skill

Disrespect vs Honor

<u>Authority is established by God.</u> To honor my authority is to humble myself and serve my leaders with a willing heart. Honor is an expression of loyalty and devotion. *There is no authority except that which God has established. Romans 13:1*

<u>Success is a reward for honoring your parents.</u> *Honor your father and mother—which is the first commandment with a promise—that it may go well with you and that you may enjoy long life on the earth. Ephesians 6:2–3*

Questions

1. What was happening and how many people were there? Daniel 5:1

2. What was Belshazzar's command? Daniel 5:2

3. What did Belshazzar's, his princes, wives, concubines, do with these vessels? Daniel 5:4

4. Then what happened? Daniel 5:5

5. How did Belshazzar respond? Daniel 5:6

6. Who did Belshazzar call for first and what did he promise them for the interpretation? Daniel 5:7

7. What happened next and how did the king feel about this? Daniel 5:8-9

8. When the queen mother/grandmother heard this what did she say to Belshazzar? Daniel 5:10-12

9. Then Daniel was called. Belshazzar rehearsed what the queen had told him about Daniel and then he made promises to Daniel for the interpretation of the writing on the wall. How did Daniel respond? Daniel 5:17

10. Daniel gives Belshazzar a history lesson. What does he tell him about his grandfather King Nebuchadnezzar? Daniel 5:20-21

11. What was Daniel's bold rebuke to King Belshazzar? Daniel 5:22-24

12. What was the meaning of the inscription that was written on the wall? Daniel 5:26-28

13. What happened that night? Did Belshazzar get a second chance like Nebuchadnezzar? Daniel 5:30-31

Answers

1. Belshazzar made a great feast and a thousand of his lords were present and they were drinking wine.
2. Belshazzar commanded that the golden and silver vessels from Jerusalem's temple be brought for them to drink from.
3. They used God's sacred vessels to worship false gods.
4. A hand appeared and wrote on the plaster wall.
5. Belshazzar's face turned pale, and he was so frightened that his knees knocked together, and his legs gave way.
6. The king, Belshazzar, called for his enchanters, astrologers, and diviners come to him. These were the wise men of the day. He promised they would be clothed in purple and have a gold chain placed around their neck, and that he would be made the third highest ruler in the kingdom.
7. The wisemen had no clue what this writing meant. So, the king was even more terrified.
8. The queen said, don't worry. There is a man in your kingdom that has insight, intelligence, and wisdom like that of the gods. Nebuchadnezzar appointed him chief of his wisemen. He can interpret dreams and explain riddles and solve difficult problems. Call Daniel, and he will tell you what the writing means.
9. Daniel was about 85 years old now. He said, "keep your gifts for yourself and give your rewards to someone else. And I will still tell you the meaning of the writing on the wall."
10. When Nebuchadnezzar's heart become arrogant and hardened with pride, he was deposed from his royal throne and stripped of his glory and was given the mind of a beast until he acknowledged God.
11. A. You have not humbled yourself.
    B. You set yourself up against the Lord of heaven.
    C. You honored false gods with God's holy vessels instead of honoring the one who holds your life in his hands. The hand that wrote on the wall was from God.
12. Mene: God has numbered the days of your reign and brought it to an end.
    Tekel: You have been weighed on the scales and found wanting.
    Parsin: Your kingdom is divided and given to the Medes and Persians.

13.   That very night the king was slain. He did not get a second chance.

Challenge

1.   Choose one thing to do to honor each parent and grandparent in your life.

2.   Say thank you ten times today.

Discussion

1.   What will pride do to your heart? Daniel 5:20

2.   What might you be doing to honor false gods above to one true God of heaven?

3.   Do you honor and obey your parents?

Self-Evaluation: Circle your heart conditions.

HEART EVALUATION	
Ezekiel 11:19-20; (19) I will give them **singleness of heart (undivided)** *and put a* **new spirit** *within them; I will* **take away** *their <u>hearts of stone</u> and* **give** *them <u>tender hearts</u> instead, (20) so they will obey my laws and regulations. Then they will truly be my people, and I will be their God. (NLT)*	
TENDER HEART	**HEART OF STONE**
Upright/joyful heart Psalm 97:11	Hardened heart Exodus 4:21; 7:3, 13...
Heart free from sin Psalm 119:11	Stubborn/disloyal heart Psalm 78:8
Sound/blameless heart Psalm 119:80	Perverse heart Proverbs 12:8
Tried (tested) heart Jeremiah 17:10	Sorrowful heart Proverbs 15:13
Whole heart Jeremiah 24:7	Fretful/raging heart Proverbs 19:3
Single heart (undivided) Ezekiel 11:19	*Foolish heart Proverbs 22:15
Obedient heart Ezekiel 11:20	Wicked/evil heart Proverbs 26:23
*New heart Ezekiel 18:31	Fearful heart Isaiah 35:4
*New spirit/new heart Ezekiel 36:26	*Idolatrous heart Isaiah 44:15
Spirit filled heart Ezekiel 36:27	Pagan heart Isaiah 44:16,17
Blessed heart Ezekiel 36:28	Blind/deluded heart Isaiah 44:18
Clean heart Ezekiel 36:29	Mindless heart Isaiah 44:19
Kept/guarded heart Proverbs 4:23	Deceived/deluded heart Isaiah 44:20
Honest/good heart Luke 8:15	Departing (Cursed) heart. Jeremiah 17:5

Good heart=Fruitful life Luke 6:43	Desperately wicked heart Jeremiah 17:9
Wise heart Proverbs 10:8	Prideful heart Jeremiah 49:16
Believing heart Acts 8:37	Exiled heart Ezekiel 11:21
Faithful heart Romans 10:6–9	Unclean heart Matthew 15:18–19
Grateful heart (grace) Colossians 3:16	Simple easily deceived heart/mind Romans 16:18

Parent/Teacher Training Tips

1. Teach the children how to humble themselves before one another by being kind and sharing.

Honoring our parents and being grateful are two excellent ways to keep ourselves humble.

---

2. Teach the children to honor their authority even when they are not perfect. God gave them their parents to honor and obey. They cannot honor what is dishonorable. But they can honor the fact that their parents gave them life, home, food, or clothes. As they honor their parents, they will be able to forgive them for their shortcomings. If not, they will tend to repeat the same shortcomings with their children.

Children, obey your parents in the Lord, for this is right. Honor your father and mother —which is the first commandment with a promise —that it may go well with you and that you may enjoy long life on the earth. Ephesians 6:1–3

LESSON 6

DANIEL IN THE LIONS' DEN

Read:
Daniel 6:1-28

Principle: An understanding spirit is an excellent spirit.
Daniel 5:12; 6:3

Who: Darius the Mede was the new King of Babylon assigned by the great Persian King Cyrus.

When: This was after the reign of King Nebuchadnezzar and Belshazzar his grandson. Then the kingdom was given to the Medes-Persian under King Darius appointed by King Cyrus, the great Persian Ruler.

Where: Babylon

Why: The next kingdom was prophesied to become the chest of silver in Nebuchadnezzar's dream. This is a kingdom less powerful than Nebuchadnezzar's head of gold. The grandson of Nebuchadnezzar had defiled God's vessels from the Jerusalem temple. That night the kingdom was taken from him.

What happened: The new ruler, King Darius, favored the elder Daniel and put him above all his administrators. The other administrators were jealous and tricked the King into signing a decree that no one could pray to anyone but him for 30 days. If they did, they would be thrown into the lion's den as punishment. They assured him that everyone agreed to honor him this way. Then they caught Daniel praying and went and accused him. The king had to throw Daniel into the lion's den. The law could not be changed. The king grieved all night for how he was tricked. He loved Daniel. The next morning, he found Daniel alive in the lion's den and punished the accusers by feeding them and their families to the lions.

Vocabulary:
Defiance is to resist or aggressively fight against something or someone good.
Defiled is to corrupt something that was pure.

Character Skill

Faith vs Unbelief
Daniel faithfully served God. *"Daniel, servant of the living God! Was your God, whom you serve so faithfully, able to rescue you from the lions?" Daniel 6:20*

Unbelief keeps us from resting emotionally. *For he that is entered into his rest, he also has stopped from his own works, as God did from his. Let us labor therefore to enter that rest, lest any man fall after the same example of unbelief. Hebrews 4:10–11*

Questions
1. What job did the new King, Darius, give to Daniel? Daniel 6:1-3

2. Could the other jealous leaders find any reason to accuse Daniel? Why not? Daniel 6:4

3. How did the other jealous leaders find a way to falsely accuse Daniel and what plot did they hatch to trap Daniel? Daniel 6:5-7

4. Why did the leaders want King Darius to issue a decree that could not be changed? Daniel 6:8

5. When Daniel heard the decree and the consequences what did he do? Daniel 6:10

6. Then what happened? Daniel 6:11-13

7. How did King Darius respond to his officials accusing his beloved trusted Daniel? Daniel 6:14

8. The officials reminded the king that not even he could change this law. So, what did the king do? Daniel 6:15-17

9. How did the king act that evening? Daniel 6:18

10. What did King Darius do in the morning? Daniel 6:19-20

11. What did Daniel reply from the lion's den? Daniel 6:21-22

12. The king was overjoyed that Daniel's God had saved him. How did he punish the false accusers? Daniel 6:24

13. How did God use Daniel's obedience and loyalty to him to glorify Himself? Daniel 6:25-28

Answers

1. Daniel was so distinguished that the king set him over all the other leaders and administrators.

2. The other leaders could find no reason to accuse Daniel. He was trustworthy and was not corrupt or negligent in any manner.

3. These leaders knew the only thing they could use to trap Daniel would have to do with tempting him to violate the law of his God. So, the plot was to get King Darius to agree that no one was allowed to pray to anyone except for him for 30 days and the consequence for breaking this law was to be thrown into the lion's den. They lied and said everyone agreed on this, but they had excluded Daniel from the discussion.

4. A decree written and signed as a law by the Medes and Persians cannot be repealed, not even by the King. They knew the King loved and trusted Daniel.

5. Daniel disobeyed the decree and honored God as he had always done. *Daniel went home to his upstairs room where the windows opened towards Jerusalem. Three times a day he got down on his knees and prayed, giving thanks to his God, just as he had done before. Daniel 6:10*

6. These men caught Daniel praying and giving thanks to God. They went to the King and told on him and reminded the king that not even he could change the law that he had signed. Daniel must be punished by putting him into the lion's den.

7. The king was greatly distressed. He tried looking for loopholes in the law to save Daniel until the sun went down.

8. The king had to give the order to throw Daniel in the lion's den. But he said to Daniel: *"May your God, whom you serve continually, rescue you."* Then a stone was put over the mouth of the den and the king sealed it with his own signet ring and the nobles did also. Daniel's situation could not be changed.

9. The king was very grieved. No doubt he had heard how Shadrach, Meshach and Abednego was rescued from the fiery furnace and hoped God would rescue Daniel. But he was distressed and couldn't sleep and didn't want to eat or be entertained.

10. At first dawn, the king got up and hurried to the lion's den. And he cried out in an anguished voice, "Daniel, servant of the living God, has your God whom you serve continually, been able to rescue you from the lions?"

11. *"O King, live forever! My God sent his angel, and he shut the mouths of the lions. They have not hurt me, because I was found innocent in his sight. Nor have I done any wrong before you, O King." Daniel 6:21-22*

12. Darius gave orders to lift Daniel out of the lion's den; there was no wound found on him. Then he gave the command to throw the false accusers, their

wives, and children into the lion's den. And before they reached the floor the lions crushed their bones.

13. Daniel 6:25-28 NIV Then King Darius wrote to all the nations and peoples of every language in all the earth: "May you prosper greatly! [26] "I issue a decree that in every part of my kingdom people must fear and reverence the God of Daniel. "For he is the living God, and he endures forever; his kingdom will not be destroyed, his dominion will never end. [27] He rescues, and he saves; he performs signs and wonders in the heavens and on the earth. He has rescued Daniel from the power of the lions." [28] So Daniel prospered during the reign of Darius and the reign of Cyrus the Persian.

Challenge
1. Look for opportunities this week to encourage others to excel. Look for opportunities to encourage children younger than you.

2. Have you falsely accused anyone? And if you ever do, what should you do?

3. Have you manipulated and deceived someone with false information?

Discussion
1. When others get promoted how would we respond if we loved them? How would we respond if we were jealous?

2. Do you have the boldness to bow your head around your friends and pray? Are you willing to receive whatever mocking or persecution this might bring upon you? Do you have a prayer routine or discipline like Daniel?

3. What did you learn from Daniel about what to do when you are falsely accused?

Self-Evaluation

Feeble Faith	
1) Prayerlessness	
2) No desire to read the Word	
3) Don't think the Word applies today	
4) Think like a Deist; God just put us here and walked away	
5) No vision for the future	
6) Eyes on temporal things	
7) Little faith-fainthearted	
8) Confusion	
9) Depression	
10) Dysfunctional coping skills: caffeine, food, pills, alcohol, etc.	

Healthy Faith	
1) Disciplined prayer life	
2) Watchful and waiting	
3) Hungering and thirsting for God's Word	
4) Longing for deeper Fellowship with Christ	
5) Saturating self with the Word	
6) Growing & maturing in faith	
7) Purposeful to develop the Fruit of the Spirit	
8) Accountable to others for good character	
9) Humbling self	
10) Serving God and being used by the Lord	
11) Steadfast maturity	
12) Wrestling unbelief and making no provisions for the flesh	

Parent/Teacher Training

1. Help the child establish disciplines in their life to develop a healthy faith.

So, mind your own business. You've got your hands full just taking care of your own life before God. Romans 14:12MSG

---

2. Teach the children when to tattle or tell on someone and when not to. There are times we "mind our own business." Then there are times we must tell an adult. We are to tell or report the facts to an adult if someone is harming themselves or another person or if they are destroying property. Teach children to look at their behaviors. Whatever is irritating them in another is something they are doing and need to correct. Judging ourselves and cleaning ourselves up is our responsibility.

    Now we know that God's judgment against those who do such things is based on truth. So, when you, a mere human being, pass judgement on them and yet do the same things, do you think you will escape God's judgment? Romans 2:2–3

SALVATION PATHWAY

1. John 3:16 What is our responsibility?

2. Romans 3:23 Why do we need a Savior?

3. Romans 6:23 If we turn from our sin, what is the promise?

4. Romans 10:9 What is my responsibility?

5. Romans 10:13 How can I be saved?

6. Romans 10:17 How can I increase my faith?

7. Revelation 3:20 Who wants to come into our lives and fellowship with us?

8.   Ephesians 2:8 How are we saved?

Obedience=love
Disobedience=unbelief
Grace=unmerited favor (a gift we do not deserve)
Faith=is believing in someone or something greater than myself.

Answers:
1. Believe
2. We have sinned.
3. The gift of God is eternal life through Jesus Christ our Lord.
4. Confess with my mouth the Lord Jesus
Believe in my heart that God raised Him from the dead.
5. Call (pray)
6. Faith comes by hearing God's Word.
7. Jesus
8. For by grace are you saved through faith; it is the gift of God.